Shattered Reflections

Shattered Reflections

CHRONICLES OF LOVE,
HEARTACHE, AND THE BATTLE
AGAINST CHRONIC ILLNESS

Merrell Cunningham

Contents

Introduction

Romance

Heartache

Miscellaneous

Chronic Illness

Thoughts

Conclusion

Dedicated to all of the boys who had no idea I was writing poems about them.

Introduction

When I started writing poetry it was my way of coping with all the things I was dealing with emotionally. The only way my brain could process everything was to write about it. I wrote poems about love and heartbreak, living with chronic illnesses, the trials of friendships, and everything you would expect a teenager to be going through. There are many people that these poems are written about, but none of them know it. I hope that people will be able to relate to what I wrote and feel it in their soul. So, now that you are joining me on my journey, I hope you enjoy it.

Romance

These poems are about young love and all of the emotions that come
with that love.

Imperfect

I wipe the makeup from my face
Baring my scars and flaws for you
I have no fear of showing it all
For you are safe and will not judge
You love my imperfections as you love my perfections

You wash out your hair gel
Letting me see your mess
With your trust I see all of you
For I am safe and will not judge
I love your imperfections as I love your perfections

Long for a Man

I long to know what it would be like
For my shoulders to be caressed by the hands of a man
To feel the electricity where our skin collides
The maturity and confidence in every move he makes
His broad shoulders embrace me
My soft cheek rubs against the scruff of his beard

I long to know the passion in a kiss from a man who longs for
nothing more than me
To feel his strength carry me
Help hold me in the trials

I long for a man older than I
To love me in a way that scares both of us to death

Heartbreak

I hadn't put myself out there in years
But for you I decided to try
You don't have a clue that you left me in tears
I didn't know that today I'd cry

I know that I'm stuck on you
This doesn't feel like a love I'll get over
Someone better is apparently with you
You're probably a great lover

Young relationships don't last
I know because I've had many in the past
Maybe in a year you'll be mine
And everything could be fine

Heck, what do I know?
It was stupid of me to open up
Love is just sitting on death row
Waiting until my time is up

I can't stop my mascara from running
I can't stop these tears from coming
Oh, how your rejection hurt
Just bury me six feet in the dirt

All I want to do is hide
Don't know what I'll do if I see you
I'm breaking down inside

Dead is my heart it has become blue

How am I to move on
How does the depression leave
Will there ever be a new dawn
Will I ever be free

Final Farewell

So, I guess I've cleaned up the mess I made when I told you I like you
I broke the ice, we're still friends, everything is well
I know that I should be happy, yet my heart is still broke
Your doofy smile I long to have looking at me
I wish that I could see you soon, I wish I was your girl
Months until you and I inevitably meet again
I made things right before we said our goodbyes, yet the feeling
lingers that you
and I are unfinished
What is to come I may not know, but I have not said my final
farewell

My Fleeting Dream

Now my newest love, you have gone and left
After awakening me from a long loveless slumber
You taught me how to carelessly fall again
How to give my whole heart over and take the pain that comes
with it
Your new world is a place I will never see you again
No longer will I have your smile to bring peace to my day
And I will hide how it hurts me, your departure
I will give up on my dream, because if I get lost in what could
have been, I will never come up for air
As much as I desire to hide the pain of you being gone
I cannot let it drown me

Talking to You

All the words in English cannot describe
The feelings that arise
When I come in close proximity to you
The closer you are the harder it is to breathe
I feel butterflies inside
I can't think about anything but you
The minute you catch my eye
I long for you so
It's hard to breathe knowing I don't have your love
The summer will be dreary until I glimpse you again
Until I am warmed by the sight of your smile that reaches your eyes
I hope the future aligns a time
For us to be together

The Princess Gets the Villain

His dark ebony hair
He pretends he doesn't care
His masterful, criminal façade
I can't help but stand in awe

Trauma in his eyes
But still, he continues to rise
He'll burn the world with raging fire
If it is my desire
Morally grey, riddled with pain
But kisses with passion in the rain

The horrible things he's done
Won't stop us from who we've become
The warmth as he touches my skin
And says our story cannot begin
I grab his flawless face
And said this time, the princess gets the villain

These Words I Write, I Write for You

These words I write, I write for you
You never fail to make me smile
Even if I've been down for awhile
Your heart is pure as the whitest snow
And you're always ready to learn and grow
My heart skips a beat when you come around
As if something once lost has been found
You are everything I want and more

These words I write, I write for you
It's a simple confession I yearn to tell
Very slowly for you I fell
I am overflowing with nervous butterflies
Every time my gaze meets your eyes
Whether or not to hide my feelings
Keeps me up at night, my head still reeling
Up 'til now I've admired you from afar
I know some may say it's a bit bazaar
I'm scared to profess how I feel inside
For fear that you will just run and hide

These words I write, I write for you
You are the greatest support one could have
You are resilient and will never cave
I aspire to declare that it's you I admire
It's you I want for ridiculous romantic things

For cheesy moments in blooming spring

These words I write, I write for you
Is it possible that you want me too?

Your Name

Right now, all I can think about is you
Over and again my thoughts engulf me
Begging of the heart, fearing of the mind
Every dream that I know will not come true
Reminiscing on the fleeting memories
Tearing my heart up over you

Wreaking havoc upon my heart
All of my friends tell me to find someone else
Really, I know I probably should
Romance never really works for me
Every glance at you I fall further
Never did I want to fall for you

Go and Smile

I am filled with anger and hurt
I want to be as far away from you as possible
I don't want to see your face or hear your voice
But then you go and smile
A smile that can light up a whole town
And suddenly I don't want to be anywhere you aren't
For this, I will never forgive you

I Want Sleep

All my mind is consumed by thoughts of you
Very little time
Escapes the sound of your voice
Right now, I just want sleep, but
Your name keeps ringing in my mind

Just a Chance

Who do I have to be
For you to want me
What do I have to wear
For you to stop and care
How do I get the chance
To put you in a trance
Where it's just me and you
And only room for two
For now, I may be a friend
But I pray It's not where we end

Life-long Partners

For as long as I can remember
You have been there
As children, we were like family
But now we are older
And while you are my best friend
I want us to be more than that
I don't want to be like a sister
I want to be a lover
You and I could be so much
Life-long partners to fight storms together
To survive trials with our love
I want to be your wife
And you to be my husband

My Confession

This is my confession to you
Though, you may never know it exists
I am so, undeniably in love with you
I am head over heels devoted to you
But you don't know how serious I am
When you tell me what you do with other girls
I desperately wish it was me not them
I want to give you everything I have
I want to be your safe place in the storm
I never want to hurt you like they do
I want to be your girl, your baby
You and me, for however far it goes

Hopeless Romantic

I long for passion and romance
To fall in love with just a glance
I long for surprise kisses and stolen stares
To be filled with a flame so rare
I long for my heart to race and butterflies to flutter
I want the warmth from your breath to make my body shutter
I long for flowers and grand gestures
A life full of adventures
I long for safety and peace
I long for you to find me

Survive it All

I could write a hundred poems, but it wouldn't be enough
To convince you that loving me could heal us up
I know that it may be a little rough
But you and I could survive it all

I just want to support you side by side
To be the place that you can come hide
I'll always be along for the ride
Because you and I could survive it all

I don't want to lie, because it will get hard
But I will never stray far
I love you all the way to mars
You and I could survive it all

Nothing Has Ever Felt...

Bright blue skies over my head
The sun warming my body
Your hand caresses my shoulder
You smile at me and kiss my lips
You are hotter than this August day
Summer love burning in my soul
I lay in your arms on a towel on the sand
Nothing has ever felt more right

The snowflakes chill my skin
Dark grey clouds above me
I'm cold where you used to warm me
I go inside my dorm room
I lay with my blanket on my bed
Nothing has ever felt more wrong

My Only Future

You're the only one I've ever seen
It's always your eyes keeping me up at night
Since I was little, I have always loved you
You are the only future I see
My north star in the midnight sky
My lighthouse when I'm lost at sea
Our whole families know we're destined to be
No matter how far I drift
I will never move on from you
Year after year I will love you forever
This summer and the next
 You will have my heart

Long Distance

I want to feel you, I want you close
I long for more than messages sent from a distance
I want your hands on my skin holding me close
But for now, I will do things from afar
And dream of the day I'm in your arms
In person for the first time

My Heart Belongs to You

The feeling of emptiness overtakes me
My heart is heavy
I should be full of joy
In this moment there should be excitement
Yet I cannot find the positivity
All because I know that I don't have you
Your love is not mine
It belongs to another
One to whom I cannot compare
While your heart belongs to her
My heart belongs to you

Showmance

It's just a show
His affection is all for a crowd
He truly loves another
I know this in my mind
But my heart has still fallen
I cannot help but feel safe when our arms are intertwined
I forget how to breathe when I look in his eyes
I could dance with him forever
I'm head over heels
Lost in the way I feel about him
He is everything I've ever wanted
But I know he will never feel the same

With You

Our differences, they are many
You come from a world of millennials
I live in a world after yours
You're full of experience
You lead a steady life
I'm still trying to find a place in the world
I don't know who I am
But I do know one thing
I'd love to figure out my life with you

Your Girlfriend

Her soul is pure
Her smile is genuine
She radiates happiness wherever she goes
She brings joy to everyone around her
She loves you in the way you deserve
You love her, because how could you not

Heartache

I've felt so much heartache the past few years, but haven't we all? I hope you are able to find something here that helps your heart.

A Mentor, A Guide, A Friend

It's been months now
Yet when the pain of losing you creeps up on me
I am still surprised by how it hurts
Some would think I'd get used to this grief
That I'd work to avoid the triggers
But sometimes it hits me out of nowhere
You were someone so dear to me
A mentor, a guide, a friend
You were safe
One of the few people who cared to ask about me
But you died and left me
And I have no one to blame
No one to take my pain out on
This grief it weighs on me
In the hardest of nights
In the brightest of days
I will keep your memory close to my heart
As long as I live you will never fade away
Your story will live on

Dedicated to Mr. John Stevens; a wonderful friend and teacher.

Grief

Grief, something so beautiful yet so heartbreaking
An experience that steals the breath from your lungs
Can repeatedly shatter the world of so many
United by the love for one person who is no longer here
The ache that fills your chest and the fear it will forever remain there
The dreams that plague you of what possibly could have been and
now never will be
The countless number of restless slumbers spent replaying every past
moment, every last word said
Maybe you knew it was your final goodbye
Maybe you thought you had a hundred more
There are moments where your world begins to feel whole
A time where the pain barely lingers
Then a reminder tears through your wall and it hurts all over again
Now look at the miracle you are going through
You got to know and love someone so wonderful
You get to feel this hurt
You got to have your life changed by a phenomenal soul
Grief, something so beautiful yet so heartbreaking

Minutes

Every few moments a hint of joy
A miniature moment with no burdens
Life feels good for a whole minute

But minutes are short
The aching sadness floods back in
I am slowly re-consumed with a crushing weight
It burns through my heart
I wish to drown my sorrows in tears
The never-ending fight to make it five more minutes
Wishing for the Fates to cut my string

Every few moments a genuine smile
My troubles are forgotten
And my pain fades away

But minutes are short
Once again, I'm in a puddle on the floor
I can't stop shaking, the pain is too real
I'd do anything to make it leave
Praying for a terminal illness to be the end of me

Save Them

Sometimes you don't know how much someone means to you until
life becomes scary
When death comes knocking at their front door and all you can do
is watch
A mentor, a teacher, a lifeline through the dark times
It's no one's fault that life comes with death
But when it is faced too soon, there are not enough tears to cry
We pray for a miracle and look for hope
We cry out "Save them!" when God is the only answer
God is the only answer

So Easy

Is it over now?

Are we too broken to be repaired?

Is your heart hurting?

Do you even care?

I was always there

Are you even aware of what you have crumbled?

A wise woman once said, "my love should be celebrated, but you tolerate it,"

And right now, that's all I feel from you

I put all the love I had to give into you

In return it was barely acknowledged

I lived for the fleeting moments of your love given

Were we a friendship or a prison?

When you see all I gave am I a thought in your mind?

Or is what I gave left behind?

I lie awake praying you give me the closure I need

Instead, a vast pit of silence is all I see

My heart is breaking in the unknown of why you have disappeared

I'm stuck in the question of if you come back could we ever be the same?

I told you how I felt and what I needed

You gave me no response

Just severed the line between you and I

The biggest pain of all is...

Why was I so easy for you to lose?

Blade

Anger and hatred towards the one who was once my best friend
A silent knife in my back
A blade I never knew you had

Fantasy Shattered

I fell too quickly
I usually know better, I swear
But the way he smiled at me
The way he spoke to me
Actually had me believing I may not get hurt
Why do I do this to myself?
Here I am in tears
Because I was stupid
I fell for you
And I told you
Now the fantasy I created in my head has been shattered
The dreams in my head weren't reality
You were but we weren't
I am real and I'm alone
Like I've always been

Forever Replay

Every word you say is a stab to my heart
My soul is swallowed in sorrow
You hurt me more than any man before
Yet you haven't actually done anything wrong
You have been nothing but truthful
But the truth hurts me more than any lie I could imagine
How easily the words slip off your tongue
How quickly they bury in the depths of my mind
To forever be replayed until I die of heartbreak

J

I loathe you
I put so much energy into you
I sacrificed what I wanted
So you could have a momentary high
You toyed with the emotions of the ones who loved you most
You had everyone wrapped around your fingers
I was under your spell
Whatever you wanted, I would've given
Whatever you asked, I would've done
I was with you til the end of the line
But you cut the string tying us together
You lost the greatest friend you'll ever have
I've waited long enough for you to come home
I'm done waiting on you

Jealousy

It's all consuming, never-ending
The way it makes my blood boil and my heart race
Something more fierce than anger
More deadly than longing
It keeps me up all hours of the night
Distracting me all hours of the day
Resisting the urge to break down in tears
Never has a feeling so strong overwhelmed me like this
Never have I felt so isolated by an emotion
I'm fighting to swim in a sea of fire
Being haunted by past and present moments
Will I ever escape the relentless flood
Into a dark, spiraling vat of darkness
Lost, with no way out in sight

Get Over You

I should not have fallen for you
You don't want commitment
You want fast and fun
But I can't not want you
You are devastatingly handsome
You are brilliant when you are passionate
I must control myself around you
You make me want to do things
Bad things I've never wanted before
You cloud my nights with dirty dreams
And fill my days with words of wonder
I don't know how to not get lost in thoughts of you
I don't know how to get over you

New Kind of Lonely

I don't know what to say
I can't find the right words to describe how I feel
It aches to know things are different
That we can't go back to how things were
I miss your constant texts
I feel a new kind of lonely
No longer hearing from you everyday
I'd fly a million miles to come and make things right
I greatly regret confessing my love
I had hoped I wouldn't lose you
But now I don't think we can go back
I love you so much
This hurts so much

I Miss You

I feel I never fully grieved you
Never was able to attend the funeral
Never watched them lower you into the ground
I think about you every day
Wondering if you would be proud
I wish you were here to see every accomplishment
Every grand adventure I take
I want to see you smile as I do something great
I wish you had lived to one day see me married
So many un-asked questions
So many experiences un-had
I miss you, I always will

Burning Flames

Wrapped up in each other's arms
Madly in love with each other
I never thought this would end
But slowly you started to drift
Further and further away you went
I was left crying in the rain
While you just drove away from me
For years I waited for you to love me
Then you finally did
But we ended in burning flames
You pushed me away when you needed me most
I would've been there for you
I will always love you
I will be here waiting for you

My Never-Ending Fit

I feel like a child
Throwing a never-ending fit
How many times can I rehash this?
How many poems can I write?
You abandoned me when I needed you
All I asked was to be treated right
Like a human who had value
I went through hell with you
I lost mental stability over you
I don't know how to live without you
I almost text you all the time
But then I remember I can't
Just the chance to talk it over
It's all I want now
Just some closure
A final goodbye
So, I can move on and start again
Maybe even find a new best friend

Not Enough

Loyal and stable
Emotionally available
Madly in love with me

Always there, right on time
You just want to be called mine
With eyes as beautiful as the moon

Always my best friend
Together until the end
I love you, but not enough

A Moment

I attach to those I know I shouldn't
For years they are a piece of my soul
Too old to ever love me like I love them
So close I can breathe them in
But I can only ever keep them for a moment
A moment that never lasts long enough

Miscellaneous

These next two poems of mine don't fit into any category. They are
each their own thing.

Vampire

Your skin is as pale as the moon
Your touch as cold as the frozen tundra
Excitement runs through my blood
You lean your head to the side
Then sink your teeth in my veins

My Sincerest Apology

I cannot find the words
I do not know how to amend what I've done
I was foolish and ignorant
I betrayed your trust and hurt you
I don't know if you can ever truly forgive me
But this is my sincerest apology
If I could take it back, I would
I know time cannot be reversed
For the rest of my life, I will feel this guilt
You will never be the same
I hope I have not ruined your life
I pray you can forgive me
I'm sorry
I'm sorry
I'm sorry

Chronic Illness

In 2020 I was diagnosed with my first chronic illness. As of right now I have Postural Orthostatic Tachycardia Syndrome, hypermobile Ehlers Danlos Syndrome, and hypothyroidism. These poems are my experience with these illnesses and depression and anxiety.

Scars

The knife gently cuts through my skin
Again, I am scarred in the name of better health
My body becomes nothing more than a pot, broken and mended
continuously
Torn flesh, bloody and bruised
Surgical marks, each with a sad story behind them
What will I be in years to come?
Will there be more marks than pure unaltered skin?
How many times will I lay under the scalpel to save me from my
body's corruption?
I look at and examine my body
I grieve the beauty that has been stolen
I sit in the pain and fear that comes from healing
Will this wound be sealed?
Will it rip open making an even bigger scar?
Will I one day be comfortable in my torn-up body?

Depression

Why does my depression overrun every waking thought in my mind?
Why do I always sink back into the darkness,
When I see a glimmer of hope?
Why does the world only ever show me the bad,
When I search for the good?
I struggle every day to escape the vast pit in my soul.
I fight to see the light in the world.
I fight to live in joy, but it only ever lasts a moment.
I'm lost, I'm heartbroken, and I'm alone.

Chronically Losing

I'm exhausted all day, but I can't sleep at night
All this pain in my body I know is not right
Tired and breaking but they say I gotta fight
When oh when will this suffering be out of sight
I just want to find a way to the light

My Mind

The demons in my mind never quiet
The intrusive thoughts never stop shouting
My mind is a prison I cannot escape
I just want to be let out of my cell

Brain Fog

A dark and thick fog surrounds my thoughts
Black cumulonimbus clouds holding my mind hostage
My eyes slowly taking in information
My words coming out wrong and confused
Should I stop, am I stuck, it comes out as stocked
My tongue is a snake not obeying my blurry thoughts
If you tell me something as my mind is frozen
I can guarantee you I will not remember it when my world becomes
clear
I apologize if I seem uninterested in what you are saying
My brain is just slowly processing what you are saying
One day, I pray I'll have a clear mind, but for now I'll hide in the fog

World's Darkness

Why am I consistently fighting my mind to see the good in the world?
My mind is always shouting the negative things at me
I can't enjoy a moment or pause and find peace
The second I slow down I feel a longing for death
I know there is good out there
I've seen it and felt it
But those moments are a dim light in the world's darkness

Sorry Not Sorry for My Life of Pain

Laying down, bed bound, losing track of time
Breaking down, hiding out, losing friends of mine
And last time I checked
My body's a wreck
But my heart and soul
Still feel it all

I'm sorry if you thought I didn't care
I'm sorry if I wasn't there
My body is breaking down
And I know I won't be found

To the world I am a mystery
With way too much medical history
Not complicated enough to die
But too complicated for them to try
I'm sorry I complain too much
But I'm 17 with a cane as my crutch

I'm sorry I have so many excuses
I swear I'm not just a recluse
My body has me living in agonizing pain
Constantly feeling like I've been hit by a train
I swear I'm not just lazy
The fact that I can't help or clean drives me crazy

I'm sorry my clouded brain impairs the way I communicate
It's taking all of me just to remember the date
Sure yesterday, I could dance and was fine
But my body and mind can crumble in short time

I'm sorry if I fear every new symptom that appears
I don't know if I will now be living with it for years
It's an endless cycle of needing doctors to get to doctors but I don't
have doctors to get into the doctors because I can't get into the
doctors without what I don't have...

I'm sorry if that was too much to understand...
It's too much for me to understand

I'm sorry if my pain is inconvenient for you
I make plans as well, like doing the laundry, but they fall through
I'll be motivated in the beginning
Then in a matter of minutes my head is spinning

I'm sorry if I'm not who I used to be
I, too, miss the old me
Mourning the life I dreamed I'd have
Getting used to the life I've been given to live

I'm sorry if I disappoint you
I feel like a failure too
My shoulders are heavy with the weight of knowing I am a burden
to everyone who dares to care about me
Of this weight there is no relief

I'm sorry... I'm not sorry... I'm sorry my life of pain got in your way

Laying down, bed bound, losing track of time
Breaking down, hiding out, losing friends of mine

And last time I checked
My body's a wreck
But my heart and soul
Still feel it all

Thoughts

The final section of this book is full of poems that describe the thought processes in my brain. They go all over the place.

Two Side

Daeva:
So much to do, burdens weighing down
Like rocks falling to the ground
You break and you fail
No knowledge to unveil

Liridona:
Chasing all of my passionate dreams
Letting out my bottled-up screams
Not caring what the critics think
Sipping my freedom like a cold drink

Daeva:
Put on the perfect face
Or you will be the one they replace
Smile through the blinding pain
They won't understand if you explain

Liridona:
Break the walls let people in
A new story is coming it's time to begin
Challenges will rise
But in the end, you'll be wise

Daeva:
The pain is too much for you to keep going
Don't go out, you're too slowing
They no longer want you

You don't even belong in a zoo

Liridona:
You can do this, you are strong
Even in times when you are wrong
So, look at the sun
And go have your fun

By the Water

Take me to the lakes
A place where I can live for the hope of it all
So, there's time for me to draw stars around my scars
If you never bleed, you're never gonna grow
But by the water the pain won't be for evermore
By the water the long story is short, and I survived

Take me to the lakes
On the road less traveled on
Where I can dive headfirst, fearlessly into life
Breathe in, breathe through, breathe deep, breathe out
By the water I'm no longer lost in the labyrinth of my mind
By the water I know peace, all too well

Inspired by lyrics written by Taylor Swift and her team

Longing for My Past

The moments I once knew as yesterday
Drift far away to a decade ago
The spirit of a child no longer here to stay
The adult life is now all I know
Responsibilities, anxieties
Never enough time, never enough sleep
When will the time come to take care of me?
Dreams of playing a princess trapped in a tower
Only to be awoken by reality
I once was a girl pretending to have superpowers
So young, wild, and free
Now a woman just working and learning
Clinging to hope that one day it'll be easier
A time where nights won't be crying and stressing
A day where peace will last forever
Oh, how I miss my girlhood
Now eternally trapped in adulthood

My Apology

I look at myself in the mirror
While most will not see
The scars hidden within me
I will see the damage they have done
Burning in me hotter than the sun
I hurt you out of fear
I'm so sorry, my dear
Maybe I'm too broken to love
Is there something wrong with what I'm made of?
Are you able to forgive the pain I've caused?
To my apology, will you ever respond?

Valued or Not?

Overwhelming, overflowing, crushing sadness
Constantly being consumed by the urge to crumble
Desperately, desiring the affection of others
Craving to be cared and celebrated the same as I do others
Is it wrong to long for adoration and acknowledgment?
Wrong to want to be loved instead of lonely?
I long to know my friends fear losing me as I fear losing them
My heartache overwhelms and overpowers all happiness
Being unable to uncover the secret of if you really care about me
or not
Am I valued or not?

Where?

Where do I belong?
In a society full of cliques and crowds
Where do I call home?
Which friends are my safe place and which ones could care less?
Who notices when I am gone?
Who notices when I am alone?
Who does more than tolerate me?
Who desires for me to be there?
I know I am worthy to be loved and valued
But where are the people that see that too

My Promise

Im fighting the voices in my head
They are stronger than ever before
Leading me into temptation
Screaming at me to break my promises
To remain pure for my husband
But the voices want me to take someone to bed
They want me to strip off my clothes
And let him satisfy every physical need

My promise is a vow I hold dear
Waiting for marriage
Denying my hormonal urges
But my heart and body want me to forsake my oath
While my mind tells me I'll regret it
I want to live and be free in the moment

But I can't give in to sexual desire!
I can't!
No matter how much I want to
I need to wait for the right moment
Not a temporary fling

Way to Go

Are you happy now?
You got him into bed
Way to go
All I can say is wow
Does this feat go to your head?
Would it have been better if you went slow?
Did you even know?
That I wanted him too
And when you hurt him, you hurt me
You go with the flow
But you left him black and blue
Now your damage is all I see
You screwed him and ran
He wasn't part of your plan
You will never last with a man

You Know Who You Are

You had him
You hurt him
You had me
You shattered me
I love him
But he's broken
Do you realize the wreckage you left behind
Hundreds of dollars and hours spent on therapy
You had the man I want
You chose to break him
Now I look at this hurting being
No longer the man he once was
I want to heal but he will no longer love
I hope you know all the pain you've caused
I hope it lives in your soul

Changing the World

Changing the world,
What does it mean?
Is it saving lives
Creating technology
Or curing disease

Changing the world,
What does it mean?
Is it helping a child learn to read
Or standing up for what you believe

Changing the world,
What does it mean?
Is it picking someone up
Or writing a story

Changing the world,
I know what it means
It's a small or large action
Done to improve a life

Ending High School

It's the end of an era
Yet I feel just as lost
As I did when it begun
Out of place, all alone
Not comfortable, not welcome
Still searching for my place
I thought I had found it
I thought I had belonged
But I was pushed out
So now I look towards a new age
A chance to start over, to be someone new
I will find a new light
I still have time to find a new home

Growing

The time has come
Where I become someone new
The transition has begun
Where I am no longer the child I once was
And suddenly I am growing
Into a woman who will see the world
Who will love and who will hurt
Who will see darkness and light
I will be an adult who faces the trials of the world
No longer will I live in innocence
Naïve to the workings of the world
I will live and flourish in my new reality

Moving

When you are young
Your world is all you know
The same friends since you were three
Growing up through elementary
You cannot imagine anything different
Then all of a sudden, everything changes
You move across your nation
To a place where there is no one you know
And you are now all alone
No friends, no grandparents
All you had once known is gone

Swifties

What must it be like
To wield such power
With the swift move of an arm
Or the slight wink to the crowd
Millions of people singing the words you wrote
Tens of thousands cheering your praises nightly
You are an idol
You are a star
But you feel like a lifelong friend
Never rude or harsh towards us
Instead, you protect us
We are your fans
Your voice runs in our blood
Loyal and true, we are to you
Just as you, are to us

Moving On

The rage has simmered down
My heart is drained of tears
All I have left is the hole you left me with
The memories of you leave me longing
Longing for the best friend I used to have
I miss the things we used to do
But it will no longer hold me back
I'm moving on from you

The Future is Coming

The future is coming too fast
I feel like an imposter in my own body
I don't know how to be the adult
But I was never the child
Packing up and moving out
Putting pieces of my younger years away in boxes
Saying goodbye to a familiar, safe place
Facing everything that is to come
I'm scared to be launched into the world
But I'm excited to see who I become

The Girl from Germany

From afar you came
A gift I had not expected
You were like light from a star
Everyone was drawn to you
And rightfully so
You radiated kindness and oozed positivity
A miracle from a foreign land
The friend I never knew how much I needed
You gave more than you got
You out others first, always
You showed me how I deserve to be treated
You made me feel valued
You made me feel seen
I am forever thankful for the gift of you

Adult

I don't want to grow up
I want to be a child again
But was I ever really a kid
This anxiety has been ruling my life for as long as I can remember
Yes, I had less responsibilities
But the weight of perfection has always laid heavy on my chest
No one told me to be perfect
But I knew I couldn't be a problem
Get straight A's
Go above and beyond
Always impress, never let anyone down
When you reach the adult world there's different rules
You have to accept imperfection
Life is too hard to remain flawless
Too many rocks being thrown my way
Too many obstacles to overcome
I'm afraid I won't be able to survive these challenges
I'm afraid to screw everything up
What if I'm not ready to be an adult?

Do You Want to Live

Day in day out doing the same old thing
Does it ever get tiring?
Do you ever long for more?
Do you want to see the seven seas
Or hike the Appalachian trail?
Do you want to experience the world like never before?
Or are you happy living life like you always do?
Living in static, a never-ending haze

Endless Cycle

Why do I feel I need a partner to be whole?
Will I even be happy once I find them?
How do we know there is true love?
Can we trust it if we find it?
Why do I keep finding the wrong people?
Ones who never love me as I do them
I find love that does nothing but hurt
Yet I still chase after romance
I still search for a partner
Even though I can't find one who wants me back
Is this just an endless cycle of heartache?

Adulthood

It's terrifying, completely and utterly terrifying
Transitioning from a child to an adult
Living on your own...
Your mom is no longer always there
Longing for life when there were less responsibilities
I'm being crushed by the weight and expectations of adulthood
I'm being crushed by the toxicity around me
I no longer know my place in the world
Who will have my back and who will stab me in it?
I'm in search of a safe place, a new home

Dreams are Just Dreams

Sometimes your dreams are too big
What you have always longed for is not meant to be
Maybe staying close to home is as far as you can go alone
The world is big, and someday, you may see it
But now isn't always the right time
Taking the safe path isn't shameful
It's okay to admit that dreams are just dreams

Muzzle On

You say let him choose
I cannot make a move
For fear of hurting you
Liking the same guy is tricky
But why should I change what I do
Because you aren't strong enough
To take what you want
You tell me to put a muzzle on
That I'm not allowed to say what I feel
All so you can have a chance with him
When I liked him first
Please don't do this to me
I don't want to pick sides

Sidelines

Here I am again
Second best as I was before
Always the understudy
Never the star
I want my time in the spotlight
But I will still applaud you from the sidelines
I will put on a smile
As I watch you shine
While I am secretly longing to be center stage
To have a crowd believing in me
I want to feel talented
But next to you, I pale in comparison
Next to you, I am nothing

Weight

"Oh my gosh, you look amazing!"
They say to me
"Did you lose weight?"
Why yes, I have
But did I not look amazing before?
Did 20 pounds really change me so much?
I looked beautiful before
And when I inevitably gain it all back
I will still be beautiful

Look to Tomorrow

I look to tomorrow
I look for hope
I look for promise
I keep going on
For my dreams of the future
For what I wish to make true
My job is not done yet
My life is not finished
I still have more to do

Conclusion

Now that you've seen into the darkest and lightest parts of my mind, I hope you are able to take something away from it. Never be afraid to write down your thoughts and make them into something new.
All my love,
Merrell

Acknowledgements

First, I want to thank my parents Ben and Shannon Cunningham. Thank you for always being there and supporting me. You encourage me to chase my dreams, and you make me feel like I can accomplish anything I put my mind to. Thank you for always letting me have a place to cry and feel safe. Thank you for always being there.

Next, I would like to thank my English teacher, Wendy Thompson. You have helped me greatly with my writing over the years. You have always pushed me to be better and go farther. You have inspired me so much, and for that I am forever thankful.

Lastly, I would like to thank everyone I wrote poems about. If it wasn't for you, I never would have been able to create this book. You broke my heart and brought me back to life. If you read this book and think one of these poems is about you, ask me, and I will let you know.

Merrell Cunningham lives in Idaho in the United States. She has been writing poetry for as long as she can remember. She has multiple chronic illnesses which inlcude POTS and hEDS.. She is a Christian and her faith plays a big part in her life. She also loves her three cats Sunshine, Betty, and Dorothea.

Author Merrell Cunningham
Photo by Shannon Sheree Photography